Lucretia Mott

A Photo-Illustrated Biography
by Lucile Davis

Content Consultant:
Andrea Libresco
Department of Curriculum and Teaching
Hofstra University

Bridgestone Books
an imprint of Capstone Press

Fast Facts about Lucretia Mott

- Lucretia was an abolitionist leader. An abolitionist is a person who opposes slavery.
- She helped plan the first women's rights convention in Seneca Falls, New York, in 1848.
- She helped start the Philadelphia Peace Society. This group was opposed to war.

Bridgestone Books are published by Capstone Press
818 North Willow Street, Mankato, Minnesota 56001
http://www.capstone-press.com

Library of Congress Cataloging-in-Publication Data
Davis, Lucile.
   Lucretia Mott: a photo-illustrated biography / by Lucile Davis.
      p.   cm. — (Read and discover photo-illustrated biographies)
   Includes bibliographical references and index.
   Summary: A biography of the nineteenth-century Quaker minister who
was an important participant in the causes of abolition and women's rights.
   ISBN 1-56065-749-9
   1. Mott, Lucretia, 1793-1880—Juvenile literature. 2. Mott, Lucretia,
   1793-1880—Pictorial works—Juvenile literature. 3. Feminists—United States—
   Biography—Juvenile literature. 4. Women abolitionists—United States—Biography—
   Juvenile literature. 5. Quakers—United States—Biography—Juvenile literature.
   [1. Mott, Lucretia, 1793-1880. 2. Women abolitionists. 3. Abolitionists.
   4. Feminists. 5. Women—Biography.] I. Title. II. Series.
   HQ1413.M68D39   1998
   305.42'092—dc21
   [B]
                                                                    97-41652
                                                                      CIP
                                                                      AC

Editorial credits: Editor, Greg Linder; cover design, Timothy Halldin; photo research, Michelle L. Norstad

Photo credits: Archive Photos, cover, 4; Corbis-Bettmann, 16; Friends Historical Library of Swarthmore College, 6, 8; The National Portrait Gallery, Smithsonian Institution, 10, 18, 20; Seneca Falls Historical Society, 14; Sophia Smith Collection, Smith College, 12

Table of Contents

Equal Rights Leader

Lucretia Coffin Mott was a Quaker. Quakers believe men and women are equal. Quakers are pacifists. A pacifist is a person who believes that war is wrong. Quakers follow the teachings of Jesus Christ.

Women had few rights during Lucretia's lifetime. For example, women could not vote. Lucretia believed that all people should have the same rights.

Lucretia became a Quaker minister. A minister is a person who leads church services. She began to preach against slavery. Soon she was preaching that all people needed equal rights.

Lucretia spent her life trying to help people. She helped start the fight for women's rights. She spoke out against slavery. Lucretia also formed a group that worked for peace.

Lucretia Mott believed all people should have the same rights.

Nantucket Quaker

Lucretia was born January 3, 1793. Her father's name was Thomas Coffin Jr. Thomas was a ship's captain. Her mother's name was Anna Folger Coffin. Anna was a shopkeeper. The family lived on an island called Nantucket. The island is part of the state of Massachusetts.

Lucretia had four sisters and one brother. All of the children attended a Quaker school. After school, Lucretia helped her mother with household chores. She also helped in her mother's shop.

At age 13, Lucretia began attending a Quaker boarding school. A boarding school is a school away from home. Students live there during the school year. Lucretia was an excellent student.

The Coffin family lived on an island called Nantucket.

Teaching and Marriage

Lucretia became an assistant teacher at the boarding school. One of the teachers was James Mott. James and Lucretia became friends.

Lucretia advanced to the position of teacher. She learned that male teachers were paid more than females. She knew this was not fair. But she was not able to do anything about it.

Lucretia's family moved to Philadelphia, Pennsylvania. She left the boarding school to live with her parents. Lucretia liked Philadelphia. But she missed James.

Lucretia's father asked James to work for him. This made both Lucretia and James happy. They married in 1811.

Lucretia married James Mott in 1811.

Lucretia's Gift

Lucretia and James lived with her family to save money. In 1815, her father died. Lucretia opened a school and became a teacher again. She helped make money for the family.

Lucretia's first child was a girl. Two years later, she had a boy. But her son died when he was just a baby. Lucretia was very sad. She did not talk about her sadness for a year. One day, Lucretia spoke at a Quaker meeting. This helped her begin feeling better.

Lucretia began speaking often at Quaker meetings. People encouraged her. They told her she had a gift for speaking. Other Quaker groups asked her to speak. Lucretia became a Quaker minister in January of 1821.

People told Lucretia she had a gift for speaking.

Against Slavery

The Motts believed that slavery was wrong. James quit his cotton trading business in 1830. He did this because cotton farmers owned slaves.

Lucretia started speaking out against slavery. She spoke at an anti-slavery meeting in Philadelphia. Abolitionists from many states attended this meeting. An abolitionist is a person who opposes slavery.

In 1840, abolitionists voted to send Lucretia to another meeting. This was an anti-slavery meeting in London. Men who attended this meeting would not let women speak. They would not even let women sit with the men.

Lucretia was unhappy about the way the men ran the meeting. Another woman at the meeting was also unhappy. Her name was Elizabeth Cady Stanton. Elizabeth and Lucretia decided women should hold their own meeting. At this meeting, women could talk about how to gain their rights.

Lucretia began speaking out against slavery.

For Women's Rights

Lucretia began speaking about women's rights. At the time, women could not own property. They could not vote or sue people in court. Most colleges did not accept women as students. College is a school people go to after high school.

Lucretia and Elizabeth held the first women's rights convention in 1848. A convention is a meeting for people with the same interests. About 300 men and women attended the convention. They held the convention in Seneca Falls, New York.

Lucretia helped write a paper called the Declaration of Sentiments. This paper said that women should have the same rights as men. It said that women should have the right to vote. Many people at the convention signed the paper. But women still did not have these rights.

Elizabeth Cady Stanton helped Lucretia plan the first women's rights convention.

War and Peace

James retired in 1861. He and Lucretia had been married for 50 years. The Motts' home was a safe place for escaped slaves. The Motts fed the slaves and gave them clothes. The slaves then traveled to Canada to gain their freedom.

Helping escaped slaves was against the law. Some people were angry at the Motts for helping the slaves.

The slavery question split the United States. The Southern states wanted slavery to remain legal. Many people in Northern states wanted slavery banned. War began when 11 Southern states formed a new country. The war was called the Civil War (1861-1865).

The Motts opposed all war. But they fed black soldiers who camped near their home. James and Lucretia helped form the Pennsylvania Peace Society in 1866. This group worked for peace.

Some people were angry at the Motts for helping slaves.

Peace and Education

Lucretia helped start a school for former slaves after the war. She helped form an equal rights group. This group fought to gain equal treatment for all people.

Lucretia and James also worked to start a new college. Men and women would attend this college together. The school was called Swarthmore College. James died shortly before the school was finished. Lucretia took his place at the opening of the college in 1868.

Lucretia spent the last 10 years of her life speaking for peace. She became president of the Pennsylvania Peace Society in 1870. She was honored for being an anti-slavery leader in 1875.

Lucretia spent the last 10 years of her life speaking for peace.

A Leader Remembered

Lucretia attended the 30th anniversary of the first women's rights meeting. She gave a long speech about women's rights. The year was 1878. It was her last public speech.

Lucretia died at her home on November 11, 1880. She was 87 years old.

Today, people remember Lucretia Mott as a leader who worked for change. She worked to change laws that allowed slavery. She worked to gain rights for women. She worked to put an end to war.

Lucretia's hard work was rewarded 40 years after her death. In 1920, Congress passed the 19th Amendment to the Constitution of the United States. Congress makes laws for the United States. The 19th Amendment gave women the right to vote.

People remember Lucretia Mott as a leader for change.

Words from Lucretia Mott

"We deem it our duty . . . to manifest our abhorrence of the flagrant injustice and deep sin of slavery."
—From the constitution of the Philadelphia Female Anti-Slavery Society, which was formed in 1833; Lucretia Mott co-authored this constitution.

"I have long wished to see woman occupying a more elevated position."
—From a speech called "Discourse on Women," given in Philadelphia in 1849.

"Let us remember in our trials and discouragements, that if our lives are true, we walk with angels—the great and good who have gone before us."
—From an 1865 speech to the American Equal Rights Association.

Important Dates in Lucretia Mott's Life

1793—Born January 3 in Nantucket, Massachusetts

1811—Marries James Mott

1821—Becomes a Quaker minister

1833—Speaks to abolitionists in Philadelphia

1840—Meets Elizabeth Cady Stanton at an anti-slavery meeting in London

1848—Helps Elizabeth Cady Stanton plan the first women's rights convention in Seneca Falls, New York

1849—Delivers a famous speech called "Discourse on Woman"

1866—Helps start the Pennsylvania Peace Society

1868—Husband James dies

1870—Becomes president of the Pennsylvania Peace Society

1878—Speaks at the 30th anniversary of the first women's rights meeting

1880—Dies at her home near Philadelphia on November 11

Words to Know

abolitionist (ab-uh-LISH-uh-nist)—a person who opposes slavery

boarding school (BOR-ding SKOOL)—a school away from home; students live there during the school year

college (KOL-ij)—a school people go to after high school

convention (kuhn-VEN-shuhn)—a meeting for people with the same interests

pacifist (PASS-uh-fist)—a person who believes that war is wrong

Read More

Bryant, Jennifer Fisher. *Lucretia Mott: a Guiding Light.* Grand Rapids, Mich.: William B. Eerdmans Publishing Company, 1995.

Harvey, Miles. *Women's Voting Rights.* Cornerstones of Freedom. Chicago: Children's Press, 1996.

Johnston, Norma. *Remember the Ladies: The First Women's Rights Convention.* New York: Scholastic, 1995.

Useful Addresses and Internet Sites

National Women's Hall of Fame
Director
P.O. Box 335
Seneca Falls, NY 13148

Women's Rights National Historical Park
136 Fall Street
Seneca Falls, NY 13148

Lucretia Mott Page
http://www.oll.temple.edu/ih/IH52/Enlightenment/Mott/MottSet.html
Memoranda on Herself
http://www.quaker.org/mott/
Women's History Month Collaborative Encyclopedia
http://socialstudies.com/mar/womenlinks.html

Index

JB MOTT D
Davis, Lucile
Lucretia Mott

$19.93

DATE			